The Bedouin

The Bedouin

Shelagh Weir

Published for the Trustees of the British Museum by
BRITISH MUSEUM PUBLICATIONS

Published by British Museum Publications Ltd
46 Bloomsbury Street, London WC1B 3QQ

First published 1976 by the World of Islam Festival Publishing Co. Ltd
New edition 1990

British Library Cataloguing-in-Publication Data

Weir, Shelagh
  The Bedouin.—New ed.
  1. Bedouin
  I. Title
  956.004927

ISBN 0 7141-2502-4

Set in Palatino by Tradespools Ltd, Frome, Somerset
and printed by Butler & Tanner Ltd, Frome, Somerset

The system used will be clear to those familiar with Arabic. I have attempted to represent the bedouin terms as pronounced, although there is great variation even in south Jordan. *Qaf* when transliterated as *g* is pronounced as in *game*.

Cover Roasting coffee beans in an iron ladle, Abu Rabiyah bedouin, Negev desert. *Photo: Shelagh Weir 1967.* Background: detail of a rug, Dhiyabat bedouin, south Jordan. *1974 AS29 6*

This page Bedouin in south Jordan.
Photo: Shelagh Weir 1975

Contents

Foreword

This book focuses on the traditional material culture of the bedouin and its significance in their daily life. It is the second edition of a book originally published to coincide with the 'Nomad and City' Exhibition which opened at the Museum of Mankind in April 1976 as part of the World of Islam Festival. A variety of bedouin artefacts were exhibited; these, and the information about them provided in this book, were mostly acquired during several short visits I made to Jordan between late 1974 and late 1975 in preparation for the exhibition. Most of my research and collecting was done among the Ḥuwayṭāt bedouin in south Jordan. Other information derives from interviews with craftsmen in Jordanian and Syrian towns, and from visits in 1967 and later to the bedouin of the Negev desert in Israel. The text of this new edition of the book remains substantially the same as the first, apart from minor changes and additions and the inclusion of some new photographs.

So much has been published on the bedouin during the past fifteen years that it is impossible to update the original extensive bibliography. This has therefore been replaced by a shorter, up-to-date bibliography of the most important and accessible works on the bedouin.

I would like to repeat my thanks to the various individuals and institutions who contributed to this project in the 1970s with their advice and help. My visits to Jordan were financed almost entirely by the World of Islam Festival Trust; air tickets were provided by the Government of Jordan; and local transport was provided by the Jordanian Ministry of Tourism and Antiquities. Special leave of absence to conduct the field work was granted by the Trustees of the British Museum.

In Jordan, Muhammad Isa of Wadi Musa was an unfailingly helpful guide and research assistant during visits to bedouin encampments; much of the information on jewellery was collected in Amman in collaboration with Widad Kawar; and Ian Dunn provided help and support in the field as well as during the preparation of the original manuscript. Clinton Bailey, Fidelity and William Lancaster, Gillian Lewando-Hundt and Emanuel Marx kindly discussed material with me, or commented on the text or bibliography, and I am also grateful to Emanuel Marx for introducing me to bedouin in southern Sinai. Above all, I would like to thank the many bedouin who welcomed me so warmly and hospitably into their desert homes and patiently answered my questions.

Fig. 1 Bedouin woman in the Negev desert, early 20th century.

7

Introduction

The bedouin are pastoral nomads whose traditional way of life is based mainly on herding animals, and partly on small-scale farming, smuggling, protection of trade routes and other activities.

The lands through which the bedouin roam are the vast deserts of the Arabian peninsula and adjacent regions to the north. The dominant feature of this area is its shortage of permanent water sources and its meagre rainfall. The only regions where rainfall is sufficient for intensive cultivation and the support of relatively large settled populations are in the south of the Arabian peninsula (the two Yemens and Oman), and to the north along the Euphrates and the eastern Mediterranean littoral. The rest of the area is a wilderness of stony steppe and sandy desert where permanent water is found only in scattered wells and widely-separated oases, and agriculture is sparse. This is the harsh environment in which the distinctive society and culture of the bedouin evolved. The term 'bedouin' in fact derives from the Arabic word *badū* (singular, *badawī*), meaning 'desert dwellers', a term used mainly by villagers and townspeople, less by the bedouin themselves. They proudly refer to themselves as 'Arabs' (*'arab*, plural *a'rāb*) – the term for desert nomads in pre-Islamic times, and later applied to all Arabic-speaking peoples.

The nomadic existence of the bedouin is dictated by their constant search for pasture and water for their animals. Some bedouin groups are camel herders, while others rely mainly on herds of goats and sheep, each group exploiting different types of terrain according to the physical needs and capacities of their livestock. Goats and sheep need frequent watering and grazing, so their herders predominate in the steppes adjacent to the settled, fertile areas where pasture is relatively abundant and wells are frequent and reliable. Camel herders exploit these regions as well, especially during droughts, but they are able to survive for longer periods than goat- and sheep-herders in the more arid, inner deserts of Arabia because of the ability of camels to utilise scanty vegetation and endure long periods without food or water.

Every bedouin inherits membership of a tribe through the male line. Tribes and confederations of tribes formerly inhabited and controlled their own territories, and it was through tribal membership that individuals secured access to vital pasture lands and water sources. Each bedouin man also belongs to a descent group of about twenty to fifty men which provides

Fig. 2 Woman of the Tarabin bedouin, Negev desert, 1926–35.
Photo: Grace Crowfoot

9

physical and legal protection for its members, and defends their rights to pasture and cultivable land.

The smallest independent unit among the bedouin comprises a married couple, their unmarried children and perhaps an older relative, who all live in the same tent. Several tents of the same tribe or descent group often join together in one camp on a seasonal basis to cooperate in herding activities in the same locality. Larger groups form only in response to particular social, economic or political circumstances. For example, large numbers of bedouin men gathered under powerful leaders at times of inter-tribal or international wars (as happened during the First World War); scores of families congregate for annual festivals at religious shrines, as in the southern Sinai desert; and hundreds of tents can surround large oases during the dry months of summer. Historically, all bedouin groups have constantly adapted and responded socially, economically and politically to changes in their local environment and the wider world.

A major characteristic of the traditional material culture of the bedouin is the effective exploitation of their richest resource – their animals. They consume their milk and meat; make utensils from their skins; weave bags, furnishings, trappings and, most important of all, tent cloth from their wool and hair; burn camel dung as fuel; transport themselves and their belongings on camel-back; and sell or barter their animals and their products to obtain those things they cannot provide for themselves.

The bedouin have always lived on the margins of agricultural regions populated by village farmers and town-dwellers, and in a state of mutual economic dependence with their sedentary neighbours. An important element of this dependence is the bedouin need for a variety of commodities they cannot produce themselves, and at variable intervals all bedouin come in from the desert to replenish their supplies of foodstuffs (such as flour, rice, sugar, tea, coffee, fruit and vegetables), cloth and clothing, utensils, toiletries and tools, in the markets of the towns. The villagers and townspeople, for their part, rely on the bedouin for livestock products (meat, milk and wool), since goat and sheep herding is limited in the agricultural areas.

In the last few decades bedouin life has been transformed by changes in economic and political conditions. Many individuals and groups have settled in villages or towns, and men have taken up full-time work as farmers, drivers, wage labourers, office workers or teachers. Others have resisted the supposed attractions of modern urban life and government efforts to settle them, and have maintained their families and herds in the desert, many migrating periodically to work in the towns to supplement their incomes. In the absence of economic and social security in the urban environment, they are reluctant to forsake a traditional way of life which provides a reliable and independent means of livelihood, and the attendant social benefit of extended networks of supportive fellow tribesmen.

Most bedouin now have larger disposable incomes than ever before, not only from wage labour, but from other activities such as smuggling (for example in Sinai and Syria) and large-scale camel breeding for racing (as in the Gulf). This has wrought great changes in their material conditions, and many products of twentieth-century technology have been imported into their tent lives: utensils, rugs, cookers, refrigerators, and, most dramatically, motor transport. Though camels are still herded as livestock, they are no longer important for transport purposes; it is far more common nowadays to see a pick-up truck parked outside a bedouin tent than a camel.

The tent

The bedouin tent is ideally suited to the desert environment and the nomadic way of life. From the economic point of view it is an extremely effective solution to the problem of providing shelter and privacy, utilising as it does the only plentifully available raw material – the hair and wool of animals. The Arabic name for the bedouin tent is in fact 'house of hair' (*bayt al-sha'r*), often shortened simply to *bayt*, meaning 'house' or 'home'. In south Jordan tents are of pure goat hair or goat hair mixed with wool, a cloth which not only provides shade from the sun, but also expands when wet and becomes relatively waterproof in the rain. Desert nights can be very cold, and tents are also snug and warm when the walls are fixed down and a fire is lit inside. Otherwise, the walls can be flexibly arranged according to circumstances. During the day the front wall is usually removed unless the weather is bad or privacy is required, and other walls can be rolled up during extreme heat to let the desert breezes flow through the tent.

The bedouin tent is simple in construction, therefore easy to erect and dismantle, and the tent cloth can be rolled up and loaded with the poles onto a camel (or nowadays a truck) for transportation. The main components of the tent are the roof, walls, poles and guy ropes. The roof is a rectangular cloth supported in the centre and at the edges on poles and anchored by guy ropes. The walls are pinned to the edge of the roof. The centre poles are about 2.2 m high and the side poles about 1.5 m. Tents vary in length – the longer the tent the more centre poles it has – but do not vary greatly in width.

The roof (*shgāg*) is made up of strips (*shuggah*) of goat-hair cloth, each 60 to 80 cm wide, sewn together to run the length of the tent. Most roofs are made up of six or eight strips, half on each side of the central ridge. One or two strips are usually replaced each year as they become worn. The roof can hang down at each end to form side walls (*ruffah*) or the back wall can extend round to the sides. The roof is protected from wear by wooden sockets (*wāwīyeh*) or sticks (*gatab*) above the centre poles but there is no ridge pole. At the lines of greatest strain, narrow bands (*ṭarīgah*) about 12 cm wide are sewn to the roof from front to back. These run over the sockets and poles and have attached at each end wooden V-shaped stirrups (*'agafah*), often made from a forked branch. Each guy rope (*ḥabl*) is looped through one of these, and the end secured by a simple knot which can easily be released for tightening or slackening the rope. At each end of the tent short reinforcing bands are

Fig. 3 Woman of the 'Adwan bedouin, Jordan, wearing the 'double dress'. She is standing before the patterned dividing-curtain (*sāḥah*) of her tent. One of the long sleeves of the dress is pulled over her head and secured by a head band (*'aṣbeh*).
Photo: Matson, 1920–48

13

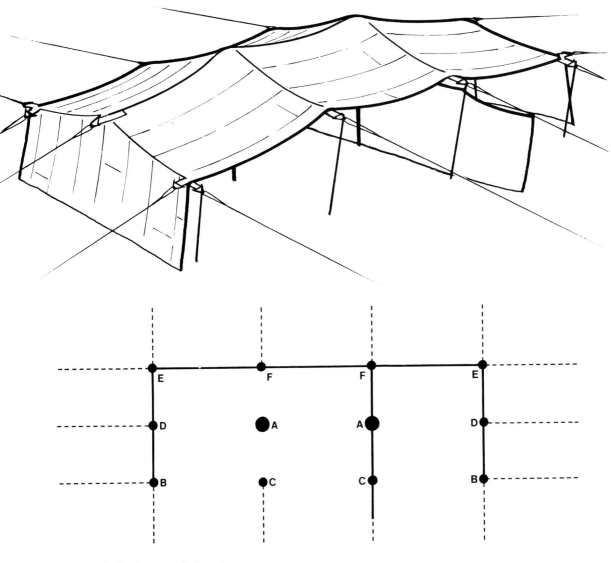

Fig. 4 A bedouin tent and plan view.

A the centre poles *wāsaṭ* D the side poles *'āmr*
B the front corner poles *yid* E the back corner poles *rijil*
C the front poles *migdim* F the back poles *zāfireh* or *mākher*

Socket (*wāwīyeh*) for centre pole.

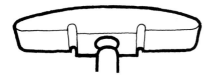

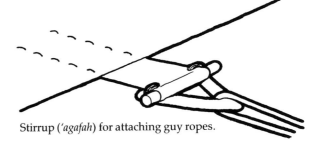

Stirrup (*'agafah*) for attaching guy ropes.

sewn along the top of the ridge to take the strain of the side guy ropes which are also attached to stirrups. The tops of the side, front and back poles, are hooked into the stirrups or fit into sockets like the centre poles. All the guys extend some distance from the tent and are secured in the ground with metal pegs (*watad*). The back wall (*ruwāg*) consists of two main strips of goat hair and wool cloth, usually with decorative cotton stripes, and is attached to the roof with wooden pins (*khilāl*) pushed through vertically. The front wall (*stār*) is made from plain goat hair and wool cloth, and is attached to the roof in the same way as the back wall. Along the front and back edges of the roof and the top edge of the walls there is often a narrow strip of cloth (*makhal*) of inferior quality which can be removed and replaced cheaply when it becomes worn from repeated pinning. The walls also have a strip (*sfāleh*) of inferior cloth or sacking along the lower edge where there is the greatest wear from the rough ground. The tent is normally divided into two sections by a woven curtain (*sāḥah*) which is suspended from the tent poles.

Body imagery is used in some of the terms applied to parts of the tent. The front corner poles are called 'hands' (*yid*), and the back corner poles 'legs' (*rijil*). The front of the tent is the 'face' (*wujh al-bayt*), and the back 'the back of the head' (*gafā al-bayt*). Other terms used are *bāhireh* for the space between the main poles and *shādah* for the area under the back wall when it is stretched outwards from the tent by means of vertical bands (*ṭarīgah*) to create more space inside. Tents are differentiated by the number of centre poles (*wāsaṭ*) they have, and vary in size according to the size and wealth of the family. Among the

Fig. 5 A Ḥuwayṭāt encampment in south Jordan.
Photo: I. G. Dunn 1975

Fig. 6 Women sewing together the strips (*shgāg*) for the tent roof, Hilalāt bedouin, south Jordan.
Photo: Shelagh Weir 1974

Fig. 7 Erecting a tent, Ḥilalāt bedouin, south Jordan.
Photo: Shelagh Weir 1974

Fig. 8 Pinning the back wall (*ruwāg*) to the roof of the tent. Ḥilalāt bedouin, south Jordan.
Photo: Shelagh Weir 1974

Fig. 9 Dividing curtain (*sāḥah*) in a tent, south Jordan. The bedding of the family is piled against the curtain in the women's section of the tent. *Photo: Shelagh Weir 1974*

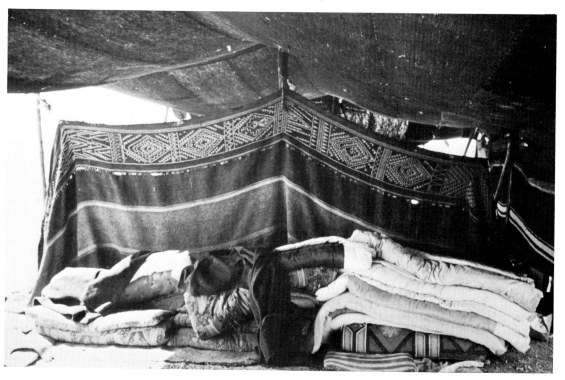

Fig. 10 Wall (*zirb*) of reeds decorated with orange, red, black and white wool. These walls are made by craftsmen in Syrian towns, and used by the Syrian bedouin and the Rwāla in north-east Jordan to create a draught-free area around the fire in the women's section of the tent. They are made by winding the wool round each reed individually before joining the reeds together with diagonally and longitudinally twined woollen threads. This is a particularly fine piece which would be considered a luxurious addition to any tent.
Total L. 7 m, H. 1.65 m. Presented by H.R.H. Sherif Nasser Bin Jamil

Ḥuwayṭāt a one poled tent is called *gaṭbeh*, two poled *fāzah* or *wāsaṭayn*, three poled *mthowlath*, four poled *mrūba'* and five poled *mkhūmas*. Most tents are two or three poled. The space between the poles is usually between 3 and 4 m, so a two poled tent is 9 to 12 m long, and a three poled tent 12 to 16 m long. The width of the tent is usually 3.5 to 4.5 m.

Domestic life

A man normally moves into a tent of his own when he gets married. He may start with a one poled tent, and enlarge it to a two poled tent as his family grows. The inhabitants of a tent are typically the nuclear family, plus perhaps an elderly female relative, for example, the mother or aunt of the husband. A shaykh will normally have a larger tent than others, a three or four poled tent, as befits his status and his role as chief dispenser of hospitality on behalf of his tribal kin group or camping unit.

The social and physical needs of the inhabitants of a tent are met in the simplest manner and with the minimum of material possessions. One requirement, characteristic of most Muslim societies, is that the two main spheres of everyday life, the public and the private, should be separated. In a bedouin tent this is achieved by means of a curtain (*sāḥah*) which is suspended between the front and back of the tent so as to divide it into two compartments. One section is the men's domain where they receive visitors, entertain guests and meet to discuss tribal affairs. The other is the domain of women where they prepare food, take care of their children, entertain their friends and where the whole family sleeps. The tent dividing wall is always suspended from the tent poles, so one, two and three poled tents are divided either into one third/two third sections, or half and half. The relative size of the two sections of the tent depends on the size of the tent and the needs of the inhabitants. A shaykh's tent will have a bigger men's section than the tent of a large family, where the need to provide an adequate sleeping, storage and cooking area is a priority.

The men's section (*al-shigg*)

If the dividing curtain is patterned, as is often the case, the 'good' side always faces towards the men's section. When male guests are present, the curtain is often extended out along the guy rope to provide greater privacy for the women on the other side. Although women are supposed to keep out of sight when their husbands are entertaining, in practice they often peer over the dividing curtain and shout comments from their part of the tent. (Their seclusion has its advantages as it provides them with an opportunity men are denied, of overhearing men's discussions in the tents of other women they visit. Thus women often have greater knowledge of tribal affairs than one would suppose.)

19

The focal point of the men's section is the fireplace. Here are kept the various utensils used for making tea and coffee, including coffee pots (*dilāl*, singular: *dalleh*), an enamel jug (*ibrīg*) for coffee grounds, a kettle for tea, glasses, coffee cups, tongs for tending the fire, and a tripod. There is usually little else in the men's section, except perhaps a camel saddle in one corner, until guests arrive. Then rugs, mattresses and cushions are brought from the women's section, where they are stored, and laid out on three sides of the men's section. The cushions are piled up at intervals for the guests to recline on.

Fig. 11 Guests seated around the hearth in the tent of a prosperous shaykh of the Ibn Sha'alān (Rwāla) bedouin, north-east Jordan.
Photo: William Lancaster 1973

The preparation of coffee

The fireplace is normally situated at the front of the tent in the centre of the men's section, and is a shallow rectangular depression with a mound at its front edge formed by the scooped-out earth. The tea and coffee are usually prepared by the host himself. Upon the arrival of a visitor, tea is brewed in a kettle and poured into a small glass with sugar, and then, if coffee is not already simmering in a pot on the fire, fresh coffee will be made. Dried camel dung and small bushes, such as the fragrant wormwood (shīḥ), which grow all over south Jordan,

Fig. 12 Serving coffee in a tent of the Ibn Jāzi bedouin, south Jordan. The coffee is always poured with the left hand into a small cup, with no handle, held in the right. On the right is a brass coffee mortar.
Photo: I. G. Dunn 1975

Fig. 13 Pair of skin bags with decorative fringes, blue beads and shirt buttons, Jordan. The larger bag (*mijrabat al-gahweh*) is for storing coffee beans, and the smaller one for cardamom seeds (*hayl*) which are used to give bedouin coffee its distinctive bitter flavour. Sometimes these bags are made from gazelle skin and called *ẓabīyeh* (pronounced *dhabīyeh*), meaning a female gazelle. Formerly these bags were ornamented with cowrie shells. *L. 80 cm. 1975 AS3 11*

are used for fuel. The beans are taken from their container, traditionally a decorated skin bag (*mijrabat al-gahweh*) hanging from a centre pole, and placed in an iron ladle (*miḥmāṣeh*) over the fire. As the beans roast they are stirred with a rod (*yad*) to prevent them burning. They are then turned out into a wooden cooling dish (*mabradah*) which is usually oval or rectangular in shape, or more rarely shaped like an animal. When the beans have cooled they are poured from the dish, which usually has a spout for this purpose, into a mortar. In south Jordan wooden mortars (*mihbāsh* or *nijir*) carved with geometric designs are the most common, although brass mortars (*mihwān*) are also used. The host pounds the beans with the pestle (*yad*) in a rhythmic beat which can be heard for some distance and advertises the presence of guests to the rest of the encampment. Meanwhile the largest of three or four coffee pots has been filled with water and placed on the fire. When the water boils, the ground coffee is tossed in, and the pot is returned to the fire and allowed to rise to the boil several times. Then a few cardamom seeds (*hayl*) are pounded in the mortar and put in another smaller pot, and the coffee is poured over them and allowed to simmer. It is then strained into a third smaller pot from which it is poured into cups. Some coffee pots have a lid on the spout, or sticks are stuffed down it, to prevent the grounds and seeds escaping. Coffee is always poured with the pot in the left hand and the cup or cups in the right. The cups (*finjān* or *finjāl*) used by the bedouin are without handles and very small, and only a little coffee is poured into each. After three helpings it is polite to indicate that one has had sufficient by shaking the cup when handing it back to the host.

The bedouin are famous for their hospitality, and it is impossible to visit even the poorest tent without being offered tea or coffee with the greatest grace and dignity. The ceremony of making coffee is not merely a way of extending friendship and giving refreshment to a weary traveller, but is in a deeper sense a physical statement of the obligation a host incurs in welcoming a visitor into his home. Henceforth he is bound by a strict code of honour to offer protection to his guest whoever he may be.

Often a host will also insist on providing food for his visitor, and will call to his wife to prepare bread and eggs. The ultimate expression of hospitality is to slaughter a sheep or goat. Meat is a luxury, and animals are normally only slaughtered on special occasions such as when there are important guests or for the celebration of a wedding or religious feast.

Fig. 14 Ladle (*miḥmāṣeh*) and stirrer (*yad*) of iron with applied
decoration, Aleppo, Syria. Used for roasting coffee beans over the fire
(see cover).
L. 78 cm. 1975 AS7 17a and b

Fig. 15 Wooden dish (*mabradah*), Jordan. Coffee beans are put to cool in
a dish after they have been roasted. This example is most unusual in
form, apparently representing a tortoise-like creature with its head as
the handle, three legs, and the open spout (through which the beans are
poured into the mortar) as the tail. This piece forms part of a set with the
mortar, pestle and lid illustrated overleaf.
L. 44 cm. 1974 AS29 15

Left Fig. 16 Mortar (*nijir* or *mihbāsh*) and pestle (*yad*) of wood with applied white metal decoration, Jordan. Used for pounding the coffee beans after they have been roasted and cooled. The pestle is knocked against the inside of the mortar in a rhythmic beat. This announces that fresh coffee is being prepared and that guests have probably arrived. Coffee mortars and pestles are carved by craftsmen in villages in the wooded, hilly areas of Jordan and Syria and are used by both bedouin and settled villagers. Terebinth (*buṭm*) is thought to be the most suitable wood both for its resistance to cracking and its resonance when beaten.
H. of mortar 28 cm, L. of pestle 82 cm. 1974 AS29 14a and c

Below Fig. 17 Wooden stopper for the mortar illustrated in Fig. 16. Used to prevent the inside of the mortar becoming dirty when not in use.
H. 24 cm. 1974 AS29 14b

Fig. 18 Brass coffee pot (*dalleh*) with stamped decoration and maker's name, Syria. Most tents possess at least three coffee pots, one for boiling water and cooking the coffee, the others for adding the cardamom, keeping the coffee warm and serving. Most coffee pots used in north Arabia are made in Damascus and Aleppo in Syria. *H.32 cm. 1971 AS2 4*

Fig. 19 Skinning a goat, 'Azāzmeh bedouin, Negev desert. Meat is a luxury food and animals are slaughtered only for festive occasions or when special guests are to be entertained. This goat is being slaughtered on the occasion of *'Īd al-Aḍḥā* (an important Muslim festival). Goatskins are used for various purposes, foremost of which are the storage of certain foodstuffs – clarified butter (*saman*) and sour milk (*laban*) – and the transport and storage of water. *Photo: Shelagh Weir 1974*

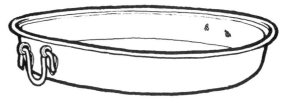

Fig. 20 *Left* Cooking pot (*gidr*) of copper lined with tin, made in Syria. *H. 24 cm. 1975 AS7 25. Right* Copper serving dish (*ṣaḥen*) made in Syria. *D. 62 cm. 1975 AS7 34*

Fig. 21 Men eating from a communal dish, Ibn Shaʿalān (Rwāla) bedouin, north-east Jordan. The dish contains twenty-four whole sheep on a bed of rice. The occasion is a grand feast given in honour of a member of the Saudi royal family for which one camel and eighty-six sheep were slaughtered. When guests are being entertained, women and children eat separately from the men.
Photo: William Lancaster 1973

The women's section (al-maḥram)

In the women's section of the tent are stored most of the utensils, bedding, food and personal possessions of the family. The
bedding – rugs (mafrash and bsāṭ), mattresses (firāsh) and quilts
(liḥāf) – is usually stacked in a pile against the dividing wall. In
this pile are also bags containing clothing and other small personal possessions, and, leaning against it at the back, woven
sacks ('idl) of grey or white wool containing grain, flour,
cheese and other foodstuffs. Along one wall on a bed of stones
will lie a row of goatskin bags (girbeh), some containing water,
others clarified butter (saman) and, in spring, yoghurt (laban).
Cooking pots and other utensils will be scattered around a fireplace, and part of a loom might extend into the tent so the
weaver can work in the shade of the roof. In some tents special
sleeping compartments (manāmeh) are made by suspending a
woven curtain (sāḥah) from the tent poles to form little rooms.
These are filled with bedding and cushions and make cosy
nests for the family to sleep in, as well as affording a degree of
privacy. A special rectangular room (khullah) is constructed for
a bridal couple from a red woollen rug.

A bedouin woman has many responsibilities and works
very hard. It is her job to gather firewood and fetch water from
the nearest well and transport it back to camp on the back of a
mule or camel in large containers (rāwīyeh) (now made from car
tyres but formerly made from camel skin). She has the everyday task of cooking for the family and, in spring, milking the
animals. Erecting and dismantling the tent is also mainly
women's work. Weaving is the hardest job a bedouin woman
has to do, and many weave their entire tent, as well as storage
or saddle bags. In addition to all these tasks she has to take care
of the children, and attempt to keep the tent in order – a diffi-
cult job when dust from the desert is constantly blowing in and
children are playing all around.

Making bread

Among a woman's most important accomplishments is the
ability to make the large thin unleavened bedouin bread (shirak). The grain is bought in the villages or towns. It is first sifted
in a circular sieve (ghurbāl), with a wooden frame and leather
thongs (bought in the towns), then ground on a stone rotary
quern (irḥah), although most bedouin now buy their flour
ready-milled. A little salt is added to the flour and it is kneaded
and pummelled in a bowl with water until it gains the right
consistency. (Formerly the bowls used for this were made in

Fig. 22 The bedouin fiddle
(rabābah) is often played to
entertain guests.
Photo: Paul de Munter 1974

29

Fig. 23 Breadmaking in Jordan, showing the wooden bowl (*bāṭiyeh*), on the right, used for kneading the dough before aluminium vessels were introduced. The woman is flouring the pancake of dough in a dish (*ṣaḥen*) while the flat pancake of bread (*shirak*) cooks on a domed metal tray (*sāj*).
Photo: Matson, 1920–48

the villages from wood (*bāṭiyeh*) but these are no longer made as aluminium bowls have replaced them). Then pieces are torn off the dough and patted into small cakes on a floured tray or mat and shaped for cooking. This operation requires the greatest dexterity and skill. Each cake is patted back and forth between the palms of the hands so that it quickly grows thinner and increases in size. When it reaches a diameter of about 50 cm it is thrown onto an iron baking tray (*sāj*) sitting on three stones over a fire. It is turned over once and is so thin that it cooks in a matter of seconds.

Below Fig. 24 Wooden bowl (*bāṭiyeh*) for mixing dough. The bowl has clearly been much used, and treasured, to judge by its wooden patches.
D. 47 cm. 1975 AS7 24

Bottom Fig. 25 Woman of the Negev desert kneading dough for bread. She is wearing bracelets (*maṣrīyeh*) similar to those illustrated in the final section.
Photo: Klaus-Otto Hundt 1975

Right Fig. 26 Woman of the 'Arab al-Hayb bedouin, Galilee, grinding grain on a granite rotary quern (*irḥah*). Nowadays bedouin normally buy flour ready-milled.
Photo: Shelagh Weir 1968

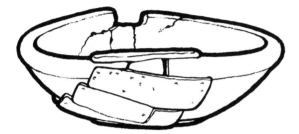

Milk products

Milk products are, with bread, the most important staple food among the sheep and goat herders of south Jordan. The season for milk is the spring and the animals are milked, usually by women, after they return from pasture in the evening. Some of the milk is drunk fresh, but most of it is turned into yoghurt (*laban*). To make yoghurt the milk is brought to the boil in a cooking pot, until recently of tinned copper (*gidr*), allowed to cool, and left overnight either in the pan with some previously-made *laban* to provide the necessary bacteria, or in a skin bag which contains enough of the culture from the previous day to turn the milk to yoghurt. Some yoghurt is kept for immediate consumption, and it is a great treat for visitors to be offered a drink from a bowl of *laban* richly flavoured with the herbs and grasses of the lush spring pastures. However, most of the yoghurt is set aside to be treated in one of two ways to conserve it for consumption throughout the rest of the year.

One method of preservation is to turn it into clarified butter (*saman*). The yoghurt is placed in a goatskin (*sa'an*) which is suspended from a tripod and shaken back and forth for one or two hours. At intervals the neck of the skin is opened and the woman blows into it (which is said to help the butter to form). Churning is one of the more welcome of women's chores. The

Fig. 27 Woman milking a goat at dusk, south Jordan.
Photo: I. G. Dunn 1975

Fig. 28 Balls of salted goats'
cheese (*jamīd*) drying on the roof
of a tent, south Jordan.
Photo: I. G. Dunn 1975

work is not strenuous and they can chat to their friends at the same time. When the butter (*zibdeh*) has formed it is removed and boiled in a pan with a number of spices which give the clarified butter a delicious flavour. It is then stored in goatskin bags in the women's section to be used in cooking.

The other method of preserving milk is to turn it into a kind of 'cheese' (*jamīd*). The *laban* is boiled then poured into a fabric bag (*kīs*) to drain. Afterwards it is put in a skin bag, salt is added and it is kneaded until it hardens. Then it is removed and formed into small balls which are laid out on the tent roof to dry in the sun. When the cheeses have become hard they are stored in sacks. *Jamīd* can be nibbled when dry, but normally it is reconstituted, for cooking, by being sieved into hot water. *Saman, jamīd* and *laban* (in season) are used in cooking the traditional dish of *mansaf* – mutton served on a bed of rice and bread (*shirak*).

Transport

It was the camel which enabled the bedouin to occupy the inner deserts and steppes of Arabia. Despite the enthusiastic adoption of motor vehicles by most bedouin, the camel retains some importance as a riding and pack animal among the sheep and goat herders of the desert fringes, and to the camel-herding tribes of the interior of Arabia. In some areas, notably the Gulf, it has also increased greatly in commercial and social significance as a racing animal.

A variety of harness can be fitted over the hump of the camel: light racing saddles, ordinary riding saddles, pack saddles, and various types of litter for women to sit in when travelling, and for brides at the time of a wedding. Many bands and trappings are woven for camels both for functional and decorative purposes. A special trough is carried when travelling to enable camels to be watered at wells.

The horse, like the camel, was used in the past in inter-tribal feuding and raiding, but in recent years its importance has been primarily for use in falconry and sporting pursuits. Horse trappings are not made by the bedouin themselves, but by specialist craftsmen in the cities of Syria.

Fig. 29 'Ajman bedouin with camels carrying all their belongings, Saudi Arabia. The large wing-shaped litters (*ketab*) are for women, and are often highly decorated. One camel is carrying two troughs,
Photo: W. H. I. Shakespear 1911 © Royal Geographical Society)

Top Fig. 30 Section of a woollen band (*libab*), Jordan. Red wool with multi-coloured patterned sections in twined weft weave, and tassels ornamented with blue glass rings. Long bands such as this are used in the Negev desert, Jordan and Saudi Arabia to decorate the camel and litter on special occasions such as weddings.
L. 11.76 m. 1975 AS7 3

Above Fig. 31 Watering camels and donkeys, and filling water skins, at the wells of al-Hinna, Saudi Arabia.
Photo: W. H. I. Shakespear 1911 © Royal Geographic Society)

Right Fig. 32 Camel trough (*hod*) with legs of bent wood and a bowl of camel skin.
H. 72 cm, D. 90 cm. Photo: Shelagh Weir (Dar al-Tifl Collection)

35

Opposite Fig. 33 Camel and rider in the Negev desert. The saddlebag is in twined weft weave and the rider is resting his right leg on the fringed leather cushion (*mirakah*) lying on the front of the camel's hump.
Photo: Shelagh Weir 1974

Fig. 34 Camel riding saddle (*shdād*) of wood with leather thongs, Jordan. The saddle is tied to the camel with woven, sometimes decorated, bands which pass under the belly. Normally a woven blanket is placed over it first, then the saddlebag, the pommels projecting through slits in the fabric, and lastly a sheepskin to make a soft seat for the rider. Saddles are made by the bedouin themselves, or by craftsmen in the villages of the wooded, hilly areas bordering the desert.
L. 51 cm, W. 48 cm, H. 51 cm. 1974 AS29 17

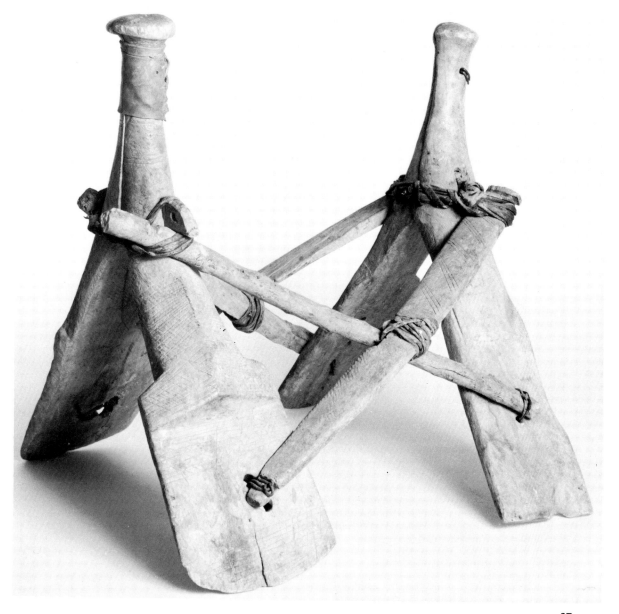

Fig. 35 Leather cushion (*mirakah*) placed on the front of the camel's hump for the rider to rest one of his legs on. Jordan.
W. 50 cm. 1974 AS29 4

Fig. 36 One end of a camel saddlebag (*khurj*) in twined weft weave in red, blue, orange and white wool with centre section in goat hair and white wool plain weave, south Jordan.
L. 2.7 m, W. 60 cm. 1974 AS29 5

Fig. 37 Camel with elaborately fringed saddlebag in twined weft weave, Wadi Rum,
south Jordan.
Photo: Shelagh Weir 1974

Fig. 38 Camel decoration (*mirakah*), Jordan. Twined weft weave in red, orange, pink, blue and black wool and white cotton. Placed on the front of the hump, instead of a leather cushion, for the rider's leg to rest on.
W. 75 cm. 1971 AS1 37

Fig. 39 Headstall (*rasan*) for a camel, Jordan or Negev desert. Multi-coloured wool in twined weft weave, and decorated with blue beads, cowrie shells, buttons and coins.
L. 74 cm. 1971 AS1 43a

Fig. 40 Bedouin hunter on horseback with his falcon, Jordan. The saddlebag is in twined weft weave. The rider is wearing the thick head-ropes (*'agāl*) fashionable in the early part of this century.
Photo: Matson, 1920–48

Weaving

Bedouin weaving is of special interest for a number of reasons. The tents and other goods essential to the bedouin are woven, weaving is the only developed craft among the bedouin and the medium for their only decorative art (apart from embroidery in the Negev desert), and the craft is entirely in the hands of the women.

Early accounts of bedouin weaving are provided by Crowfoot (1945) and Dalman (1928: Vol V). De Boucheman (1934: 116) illustrates a Sba'a loom but the drawing contains several inaccuracies. These mistakes were perpetuated by Dickson (1949: 98) who appears to have copied the drawing, though he does not acknowledge the source. Some Arabic terms are provided by Musil (1908: Vol 3, 124–5 and 1928b: 68) and Jaussen (1908: 32), who relegates the subject to a footnote. More recently, excellent detailed descriptions of bedouin weaving have been published by Crichton (1989) and Hecht (1989).

The following account of bedouin weaving is based on observations among various groups of the Ḥuwayṭāt tribe in

Fig. 41 Man shearing a sheep, 'Azāzmeh bedouin, Negev desert. Shearing is normally a man's job, whereas all the other processes in textile production among the bedouin are the responsibility of women.
Photo: Klaus-Otto Hundt 1975

Fig. 42 Woman spinning wool by rolling the shaft of the spindle on her thigh, south Jordan. In the Jordan/Palestine area, the spinning is always done to the right.
Photo: Shelagh Weir 1975

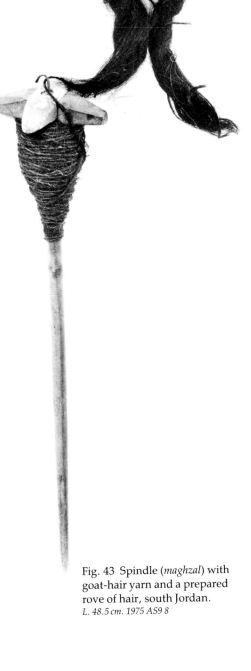

Fig. 43 Spindle (*maghzal*) with goat-hair yarn and a prepared rove of hair, south Jordan.
L. 48.5 cm. 1975 AS9 8

south Jordan, mainly the Bani Naʿīmāt, Dhiyabāt and Ibn Jāzī. A number of woven articles from Syria and the Negev desert have been illustrated, in addition to Jordanian pieces, for comparative purposes.

Spinning

After shearing has taken place, the goat hair and wool are teased by hand ready for spinning. The fibres are spun with a simple hand spindle (*maghzal*) consisting of a wooden shaft and a wooden whorl, made from a single bar or crossed bars, with a metal hook projecting above it. They are thus similar to those used by the villagers in the Hebron Hills (Weir 1970: 10), except that the shafts appear to be somewhat longer.

Before spinning, the fibres are teased with the fingers into a long *rove* twisted slightly in the direction of spin. During spinning the rove is wrapped round the left wrist or allowed to float cloud-like over the left shoulder. No distaff is used to hold the rove. The distaff does not appear to have been used by either the settled peoples or the nomads of north Arabia, though I have observed its use among the bedouin in Qatar

Fig. 44 Woman of the Bani Naʿīmāt bedouin, south Jordan, standing before a tent draped with newly-dyed wool drying in the sun. Wool is usually dyed in the yarn with dyes bought in town markets, or taken to dyeing shops to be dyed by specialists. Formerly the bedouin used natural dyes.
Photo: Shelagh Weir 1975

and the villagers of Yemen. The method most often used for spinning is with the spindle suspended, sometimes called the drop-and-spin method. The thread is caught under the hook above the whorl, and the spin is achieved by rolling the shaft of the spindle on the thigh from the knee upwards, or twirling the whorl in the fingers in a clockwise direction. The spindle is then dropped spinning, whorl uppermost, while the thread is drawn out from the rove with the fingers. When a length of thread has been spun, it is unhooked, wound round the shaft of the spindle then hooked up again. The direction of spin is always to the right (Z-spun). According to Crowfoot (1945) this is the direction of spin throughout the Syro-Palestine area including Jordan, whereas in Egypt and the north Sudan it is to the left (S-spun). This geographical difference in spinning technique also appears to have existed in antiquity. I did not observe the spinning of cotton, though the Ḥuwayṭāt women said they spun their own cotton thread from raw cotton which they bought in Maʿān market. Crowfoot (1945) writes that cotton was spun by the Bani Ḥasan in north Jordan with the spindle whorl downwards, and the spindle was not dropped, but simply rolled on the thigh as the thread was drawn out from the rove.

The spun thread is wound off the spindle shaft into skeins then dyed if a coloured yarn is required. It is then rolled into a ball and rewound into balls of doubled thread ready for plying. Two-ply yarn (*mabrūm*) is used for both the warp and the weft in bedouin weaving. Plying is done with a spindle, apparently the same as that used for spinning (called *mabram* instead of *maghzal* when thus used). When plying, the woman usually sits on the ground, and either rotates the spindle shaft on her thigh with one hand while drawing out the doubled thread from the ball with the other, or holds the thread high to allow the spindle to rotate in the air. The direction of spin for plying is, of course, to the left.

The loom (*naṭi*)

A loom is a device for maintaining the *warp* threads in tension while the *weft* thread is interwoven with them at right angles. The bedouin loom fulfills this function with a minimum of simple components, namely a number of sticks and beams only one of which, the *sword beater*, is carved for the purpose. The apparatus is specially set up each time something is to be woven, and dismantled when it is completed.

Before weaving, the warp threads are stretched in a figure of

Opposite, above Fig. 45 Bedouin women in front of their tent, Transjordan (Jordan). Note the patterned band decorating the tent roof.
Photo: Grace Crowfoot 1926–35

Opposite, below Fig. 46 Weaving on the bedouin ground loom (*naṭi*), south Jordan. Pushing down on the warp threads to obtain the shed.
Photo: Shelagh Weir 1974

eight between two *warp rods* of iron or wood (I did not observe this). The length of the loom, depends on the desired length of the item to be woven, and the width required decides the number of warp threads. The warp rods are lashed to beams, a *warp beam* and a *breast beam*, which are pegged firmly into the ground. It is very important that the warp threads be of even tension. As the warp is continuous, one long thread having been wound back and forth round the warp rods, the tension can be adjusted more easily than if each thread were tied to the rods separately. After warping, the warps are divided into two sets of alternate threads. One set, which I will call the *heddle warps*, is suspended from a *heddle rod* by means of a continuous *leash*, and passes under a *shed stick*. The other set, which I will call the *shed stick warps*, passes over the shed stick. The shed stick thus separates the two sets of warps, and they cross between the shed stick and the heddle rod.

Three basic weaving processes take place on all looms: changing the positions of the different sets of warp threads to form the *shed* and *countershed*, inserting the weft thread, and beating-in the weft thread. Many hand looms have mechanical apparatus which relieve the weaver of some of the hard work of performing these tasks. The bedouin loom has no such mechanical aids. Its operation, though simple in theory, is extremely arduous in practice, depending for its effectiveness entirely on the physical strength and manual dexterity of the weaver.

The weaving process

The weaver sits at one end of the loom facing the heddle. As weaving progresses she sits on the woven fabric which helps maintain the loom in tension. The weaving process involves inter-changing the two sets of warp threads lying immediately in front of her. The heddle on the bedouin loom holds one set of warp threads permanently at a fixed height, and is *never* moved up and down in the vertical plane during weaving to create the shed and countershed. The warp threads can only be alternated by the physical exertions of the weaver, and the operation requires strength because the rough-spun threads cling together and are heavy to handle. To obtain the countershed, the shed stick warps must be raised above the heddle warps. Reaching over the heddle, the weaver pulls the shed stick towards the heddle, then grasps handfuls of the shed stick warps and tugs them upwards, at the same time pushing down on the heddle warps. Gradually she raises the shed stick

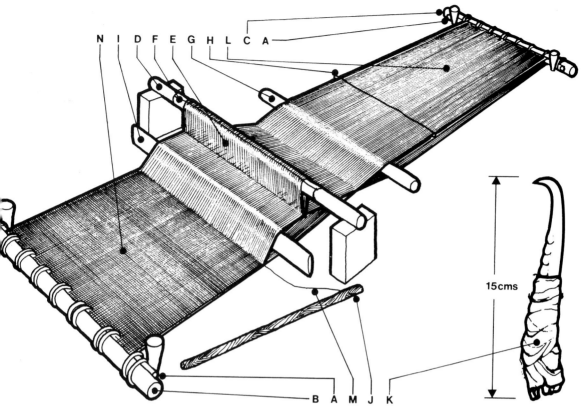

Fig. 47 Fixed heddle loom used by bedouin women. The terms are those used among the Ḥuwaytāt bedouin, and vary among different groups.

A warp rod *muṭrag*
B breast beam *gā'al-naṭi*
C warp beam *rās al-naṭi*
D heddle rod *minyār*
E leashes *nīreh*
F string securing leashes *gaṭar*
G shed stick *ḥāf, maḥāfah*

H string round upper warps *gilādeh*
I sword bearer *minshāz, minsāj, minḥāz*
J stick spool *maysha'*
K beating hook *mishgā, miḥtā*
L warp threads *sitā*
M weft thread *laḥmeh*
N woven fabric

Shedding diagram of the bedouin loom (not to scale).

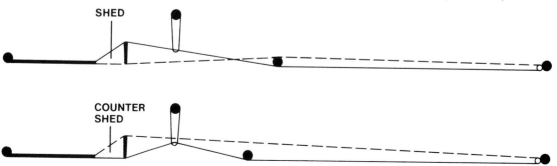

SHED

COUNTER SHED

warps above the heddle warps on her side of the heddle. Gathering the shed stick warps on one arm, she inserts the sword in the flat position in the newly-formed countershed, and, grasping each end, pulls it towards her to complete the separation of the two sets of warps and to force the 'crossing' down to the edge of the woven fabric. The sword is then turned on edge to keep the countershed open while the weft thread is passed through (the *pick*). To return the warp threads to the shed position the weaver first removes the sword, then presses down with the flat of her hand with all her weight onto the warps on her side of the heddle. She then leans over the heddle and presses down on the warps on the other side, forcing the shed stick warps down to their former position. The result is to return the 'crossing' to the far side of the heddle. As before, the sword is inserted into the newly formed shed to complete the separation of the warps, then turned on edge for the pick. As

Fig. 48 Weaving on the bedouin ground loom, south Jordan. Pulling up the shed-stick warp threads to obtain the countershed.
Photo: Shelagh Weir 1975

well as using the sword to separate the threads, the weaver also strums them from side to side with her beating hook, and prods them with her outstretched fingers. Some weavers also rub a bar of soap across the warps to ease their separation.

A pick is made, that is the weft thread is passed through the shed or countershed, by means of a simple *stick spool* (equivalent in function to a shuttle on a more sophisticated loom). The spool can be any stick about one metre long, and the weft is wound onto it in long figures-of-eight. The weft is unwound from the spool before each pick. The main implement for beating-in the weft thread is the *beating hook*, either a steel hook or a gazelle horn. It is used as follows: the weaver inserts the sword on its edge between the upper and lower warps, and pulls it up close to the fabric. This tautens the upper warps and presents them at a more convenient angle to the weaver. With the hook she then plucks up groups of these upper warps, then beats down with force towards the fabric. This plucking and beating movement is done very quickly in a series of deft movements, from one side of the loom to the other, two, three or four times, to drive the weft firmly home. As the hooks weigh very little, the success of the beating-in depends entirely on the strength of the weaver and the dexterous way she manipulates the hook.

The sword beater is usually considered to be the main implement used for beating-in on this type of loom, but in south Jordan this is not the case, and sometimes it is not used at all

Fig. 49 Weaving on the bedouin ground loom, south Jordan. Beating-in the weft thread with gazelle horns.
Photo: Shelagh Weir 1974

for this purpose. When it is, the narrow edge is beaten against the fabric with force one, two or three times before or after beating-in with the hooks.

Weaving practices vary according to personal preference or the type of fabric required. Thus beating-in may be more rigorous when a close-weave fabric, for example a tent roof, is required, or less rigorous when an item is being made for sale. Also some weavers beat-in immediately after making the pick, others change the shed first and then beat-in, and others do both.

As the woven section grows the heddle rod has to be moved, with its supports, along the loom. Sometimes when a very long piece of cloth is being woven, such as a tent roof strip, the breast beam is released from its pegs, part of the woven section is rolled up, and the warp rod and beam are anchored again. This makes it easier to keep the loom in tension and to protect the woven part from the sun or rain.

The maximum width is limited to that which two weavers working together can manage, that is up to about one metre. When an article is required that is wider, two loom widths are joined together lengthways. Such widths are usually woven in sequence along the same warp, which accounts for the frequent failure to match the designs on a patterned article. Looms can extend to twelve or more metres in length.

Pattern weaving

Most fabrics woven by the bedouin are in plain weave. For this, single alternate warp threads pass through each of the leash loops and weaving takes place as described above. The finished fabric is *warp faced*, that is the weft is concealed after beating-in and only the warp is seen. Some plain-weave fabrics have stripes and bands of colour. This is achieved by using coloured threads for the requisite number of warps. Because the fabric is warp faced, these show up as coloured bands in the final product. The bedouin also weave quite complex and extremely attractive patterns into their fabrics. The patterns are achieved by the use of two different techniques of weaving, one giving a warp-faced pattern and the other a weft-faced pattern. These types of pattern weaving are unknown among the village women of the Hebron hills and north west Jordan, who use a similar loom. However, both techniques are widespread among the bedouin in Arabia.

Overleaf, top Fig. 51 Part of a tent
dividing-curtain (*sāḥah* or *gāṭa'ah*),
Jordan or Syria. Five strips are
joined lengthways, and the
curtain includes examples of the
two different pattern-weaving
techniques used by the bedouin.
This is a particularly fine curtain of
the type often made specially as a
gift from one tribal shaykh to
another. It is possible that the
warp-patterned strips and the
twined-weave strips were made
separately, and by different tribes,
and joined together by the final
owner. The warp-patterned strips
are Syrian in style, and include
figurative designs of humans and
camels. The strips with twined-
weave designs could be Syrian or
Jordanian
*Total L. 10 m. Presented by H.R.H. Sherif
Nasser Bin Jamil*

Fig. 50 Rug (*bsāṭ*), probably
Ḥuwayṭāt bedouin, south Jordan.
Woven in green, brown and red
bands of wool, with warp patterns
in white (cotton) on brown, and
red on green. Two loom widths
are joined lengthways.
L. 2.87 m. 1975 AS3 7

Warp patterns (ragm)

Warp-faced patterns are worked in bands running lengthways
on the loom and therefore on the finished article. For this type
of patterning each leash loop carries two warps instead of one,
one of the pattern colour, which is most often white, and one
of the background colour, for example black. The warps lying
over the shed stick are arranged in pairs likewise. The warps
for the plain-weave sections adjacent to the pattern bands pass
singly through the leashes in the normal way. To make the pattern the weaver selects with her fingers one thread from each
pair of warps (at the shed or countershed position), leaving the
other one to float as a loose strand on the back of the fabric until
it is selected to appear on the surface as part of the design. As
the required warps are selected, the sword is pushed through
to keep them separate while the next pattern band, if there is
one, is worked. When each of perhaps two or three pattern
bands have been worked in this way, the selected warps are
threaded onto the weaver's arm while the shed of the plain
sections is changed, then the sword is pushed through and
turned on edge to keep the threads separate for the pick. The
weft is passed through on the spool and beaten-in as in plain
weaving.

Twined weft patterns (nagash)

Weft-faced patterns are usually worked in bands at intervals
across the width of a plain weave fabric. To make this type of
pattern the weaver uses two strands of weft thread at a time

Opposite, bottom Fig. 52 Detail of a dividing-curtain (*sāḥah*) for a tent, possibly Ḥuwayṭāt bedouin, Jordan. Woven from black goat hair with white cotton warp patterns. A third strip of plain woven wool, about 40 cm wide, is attached below these two patterned strips. This type of richly patterned curtain was made and used by certain Jordanian tribes up to twenty or thirty years ago, but is now no longer made and rarely seen.

W. of top section 43 cm and lower section 70 cm. Total L. 7.3 m. 1974 AS29 3

Below Fig. 53 Storage and travelling bag (*'idl*), Syria. Red and white warp patterns on a dark blue background. All wool including the white. The bag is made from two loom widths joined lengthways, folded and sewn up the sides with coloured wools. The tasselled fringe in red, orange and yellow wool may have been added separately to make the bag more festive for a special occasion such as a wedding. Bags such as this are used to store possessions in the tent, and in pairs, one on each side of a camel when travelling.

W. 1.14 m. 1975 AS7 4

Below Fig. 54 Two ends of a woollen girdle (*gīsh*), Negev desert. Plaited in black with narrow V-shaped stripes in red, blue and green. One end is in multi-coloured twined weft weave and decorated with tassels, and beads of bone and blue and brown glass. The other end is decorated with cowrie shells. This narrow girdle is wrapped around the waist over a wider belt made from narrow plaited strips of black goat hair and white wool sewn together to make a band about 10 cm wide.
W. 3.5 cm and 8 cm, L. 2.88 m. 1974 AS29 26

Right Fig. 55 Section of a rug (*bsāt*), Dhiyabāt bedouin, south Jordan. The background is in brown and white bands of wool, and the transverse pattern bands in twined weft weave in red, orange, dark and light blue and white wool. Two loom widths are sewn together lengthways.
Total L. 3.65 m. 1974 AS29 6

and with the fingers inserts one under, and the other over, each warp thread twisting them so as to enclose each warp. Sometimes the wefts are passed over and under two, three or even more warps at a time. The technique is essentially the same as that used in twined basketry. When a straight-sided design is worked, a slit tapestry effect results, but usually the designs are diamonds and shapes with sloping edges so that the weft can overlap and long slits are avoided. The weft is beaten-in as for plain weave.

Plaiting

In the Negev desert and Jordan, patterned girdles (*gīsh* and *shwaḥīyeh*) were formerly made by a technique which combined plaiting and weaving. The threads were plaited towards the centre and the outer strands became 'wefts' as each in turn was woven through the other threads. This process and its distribution is well described by Crowfoot (1943).

Fig. 56 Woman of the Tarābīn
bedouin, Negev desert, plaiting a
girdle (*gīsh*).
Photo: Grace Crowfoot 1920s or 30s

Weaving products

The most important product of the bedouin loom is the cloth
for their tents. The roof strips are made from goat hair, or a
mixture of goat hair and wool. In the latter case, the warp is
goat hair and the weft is wool, or wool and goat hair plied. The

front and back walls may contain more wool than the roof, which needs to be stronger and more waterproof. The back wall often has one or two decorative bands of white cotton.

The most splendid item woven for the tent is the dividing curtain (*sāḥah*). Dividing curtains with intricate geometric warp patterns were widespread among the tribes of Jordan and Syria until the middle of this century, but are now rarely found. Musil (1908: 129 and 162) illustrates two examples among the Ibn Fāyez bedouin in south Jordan. Crowfoot (1945) mentions seeing them among the Ghanamāt bedouin near Madaba and Bani Ḥasan bedouin near Jerash, and I have seen them in several tents of the Naʿīmāt in south Jordan.

Among the Ṭuwayḥā bedouin near Bayyīr in south-east Jordan, I also saw dividing curtains in white cotton with small pattern bands in the twined weft technique. The dividing curtains used by various tribes throughout Arabia would make an interesting comparative study. In Qatar large decorative panels of twined weft are woven at one end of the curtain, and in the Empty Quarter warp patterns are worked on curtains and other textiles (Cole 1975: 81–2).

Apart from tent cloths, bedouin women weave rugs (*mafrash* when plain, *bsāṭ* when patterned), saddle-bags (*khurj*) for camels and horses, storage sacks (*ʿidl*), bags (*mizwad*) also used as cushions, and trappings for camels and horses.

Textiles produced for the bedouin by town and village weavers

Many bedouin are unable to make for themselves all the textiles they need or want. The camel herding tribes of the inner deserts do not have the goats and sheep to provide the hair and wool for weaving tent cloth, rugs and bags. Also, some women are unable to weave because they lack the skill or time. Sometimes tent cloth is needed quickly, for example when a man wishes to marry and set up his own tent at short notice. In all such cases the cloth has to be bought ready-made. One solution is to buy from other bedouin who have made surplus to their own requirements. For this reason one cannot assume that any piece of weaving was actually made by the women of the tent or tribe where it is found. Fine pieces of weaving, in particular, such as dividing curtains (*sāḥah*), undoubtedly pass from hand to hand and are given as presents.

The main external sources of textiles for the bedouin are the towns and villages of the settled areas bordering the deserts. Here a weaving industry exists based partly on the demand from the bedouin for textiles they are unable to provide for themselves. The weavers are always men, and they work on two different types of loom, a vertical loom with a fixed heddle, and a horizontal loom with moveable heddles.

Below Fig. 57 Cushion cover (*mizwad*), probably Negev bedouin. Woven in twined weft weave in red, blue, white, orange, yellow and green wool. Used for storing small possessions in the tent, and as a cushion for guests to lean on.
L. 80 cm. 1975 AS3 4

Right Fig. 58 Cushion cover (*mizwad*), Syria. Woven in wool in black with a dark red stripe, and warp patterns in white.
L. 1.02 m. 1975 AS7 6

It is on the vertical loom that tent cloth is produced. Dalman (1937 Vol. V: 107), Crowfoot (1941) and Weir (1970) describe the workings of this loom. Vertical looms manufacturing tent cloth were in widespread use in Palestine during the first half of this century – in Safad, Majd al-Kurum, Samakh, Beisan, Anabta, Tulkarm, Nablus and Hebron. The vertical loom has not been used in the Palestine area since about 1948. Cloth for the bedouin of southern Palestine was also made in the big weaving centre of Shiḥīm in southern Lebanon. (Abū Muḥammad, a weaver working in Jerash in the early 1970s, related how he used to travel from Shiḥīm to sell his cloth to the Negev bedouin in Rafah, Khan Yunis, Gaza and Beersheba during the British Mandate.) When this market was cut off after the partition of Palestine in 1948, many weavers moved to Syria and Jordan. The weavers working today in Irbid and Jerash in Jordan are originally from Shiḥīm. In Syria, the vertical loom industry was still in existence, according to informants, in Yabroud, Riha, Homs, Damascus, Latakia and Tartous.

The hair and wool for vertical looms is provided locally by goat and sheep herders, both villagers and bedouin, and it is also imported from Egypt and Libya. It is spun and plied simultaneously on an ingenious hand spinning apparatus similar to that used in the Balkans. The cloth is woven mostly on commission, though if he can, the weaver will make surplus for sale in the markets. Customers of the Jordanian weavers include nomads from as far afield as Saudi Arabia, Qatar, Abu Dhabi, Dubai, Iraq and the Sudan. Usually the customers or traders come to place their orders directly with the weavers.

It is interesting to note here that until recently male weavers in the villages of north Yemen used a fixed heddle ground loom, similar to that of the bedouin women, to make tent cloth for the southern Arabian bedouin as well as rugs for Yemeni houses (Weir 1975).

Mention should also be made of the horizontal treadle loom industry (Weir 1970: 27). Rugs made by male weavers working on this type of loom in Madaba in Jordan and in many towns in Syria, are traded all over Jordan and bought by the bedouin for use in their tents.

Fig. 59 Weaver, Aḥmad Yasin Hajj Shehādi, in Irbid, north Jordan, weaving a strip for a tent wall (*ruwāg*). Vertical fixed-heddle looms such as this are used by male weavers in certain towns and villages in Jordan, Lebanon and Syria (and until 1948 in Palestine) to weave the cloth for the walls and roofs of bedouin tents. The cloth is made on commission, or is sold in the local markets, for tribes from as far afield as Saudi Arabia and the Gulf. The demand is mainly from the camel herders who have insufficient goats to make their own cloth, and from those bedouin whose women cannot weave, or who need the cloth urgently.
Photo: Shelagh Weir 1974

Costume

All the fabrics used for bedouin clothing are purchased from itinerant merchants or from markets in the towns. Some clothes, such as men's cloaks and shirts, are bought ready-made; others are or were made by the women. Some tents even boast Singer sewing-machines.

The older costumes of men and women are well-adapted to the extremes of temperature in the desert, being loose fitting and having several layers which provide good insulation against heat and cold. However, more recent fashions such as women's dresses made from nylon and other man-made fibres, are less obviously suitable for the desert environment – proving that among the bedouin, as in other societies, fashion concerns often override practical considerations such as physical comfort.

Clothing denotes social and marital status, and a woman's clothing can indicate the tribe or locality from which she comes. Bedouin costume is subject to changes in fashion, and styles of women's clothing in particular, are very different today from those of the past. Though bedouin women's costumes continue to distinguish them from their village neighbours, they are often influenced by village fashions, especially in the Negev region where there is substantial economic and social interaction between the two communities.

Women's costume

Until about the 1940s, the bedouin women of the Jordan valley area and the region to the east wore an extraordinary dress of enormous proportions – three or more metres in height, and with pointed 'winged' sleeves up to two metres long. In the nineteenth century this style of dress was made from hand-woven cotton or from machine-made cotton imported from Manchester, both materials dyed a light or mid indigo-blue. This century dark blue and later black cottons were favoured. This was not the dress of a giantess, as one might suppose, but was a combination of dress, underdress and veil. A girdle (shwaḥīyeh) of plaited wool was tied over the dress and around the waist, and the material was pulled up and through the belt until the hem was level with the ground and the excess material fell in a baggy fold. This fold was called the 'ob, and the dress was called thōb 'ob or khalagah. The points of one or both sleeves were thrown over the head as a veil and secured with a band ('aṣbeh), often, for best wear, made of fine brocaded silk.

Fig. 60 Bedouin of Palestine wearing a voluminous sleeveless cloak ('abāyah) of striped woven wool, made in the cities by male weavers and worn by the bedouin of north Arabia. A similar cloak of finer wool or cotton without stripes, and with metal thread embroidery at the neck, is worn by shaykhs and others for special occasions. Early twentieth century.

Sometimes the dress had some simple embroidery in zig-zag lines (*'irayjeh*) on the front.

Women say they favoured this cumbersome dress for reasons of modesty – 'because it hid the body well'. There was also a status aspect, for the extravagant use of material was a form of conspicuous consumption, and it was desirable to have a fold which fell close to the hem, showing that the maximum amount of cloth had been used.

Similar dresses are still worn by older women in the towns of Al-Salt and Jericho, those of Jericho decorated with vertical bands of brightly-coloured cross-stitch embroidery. However, the bedouin women of Jordan no longer wear the *thōb 'ob*, preferring normal-sized dresses in satins and man-made fibres.

Fig. 61 Woman of the 'Arab al-Hayb bedouin, Galilee, embroidering a panel for the skirt of a dress (*shursh*). She is wearing a black crepe head veil (*milfa'*), a silk and metal brocade head band (*'aṣbeh*) and gold coins (British sovereigns) round her forehead.
Photo: Shelagh Weir 1968

Tent and loom of the Bani Naʿīmāt bedouin, south Jordan. *Photo: Shelagh Weir 1974*

Sleeping compartments (*manāmeh*) in the women's section of a tent of the Bani Naʿīmāt bedouin, south Jordan. *Photo: Shelagh Weir 1975*

III. Pounding coffee beans in a wooden mortar (*mihbāsh*), south Jordan. *Photo: Shelagh Weir 1974*

IV. Churning butter in a goatskin (*sā'an*) suspended from a tripod, Bani Na'īmāt bedouin, south Jordan. *Photo: Shelagh Weir 1975*

. Baking bread (*shirak*) on a convex metal tray (*sāj*), Bani Naʿīmāt bedouin, south Jordan. *Photo: Shelagh Weir 1975*

VI. Women of the Bani 'Ataynah bedouin singing two-part songs at a wedding, south Jordan. *Photo: Shelagh Weir 1974*

Left VII. Woman of the 'Arab al-Hayb bedouin, Galilee. *Photo: Shelagh Weir 1968*

Right VIII. Woman with tattoos and dress with embroidered chest panel, Negev desert. *Photo: Shelagh Weir 1968*

Plying woollen thread to make a two-ply yarn for weaving, Bani Naʿīmāt bedouin, south Jordan. *Photo: Shelagh Weir 1975*

X   Weaving a warp patterned rug (*bsāt*), Bani Na'īmāt bedouin, south Jordan. *Photo: Shelagh Weir 1974*

Selecting the warp threads to make the pattern on a rug (*bsāṭ*). *Photo: Shelagh Weir 1975*

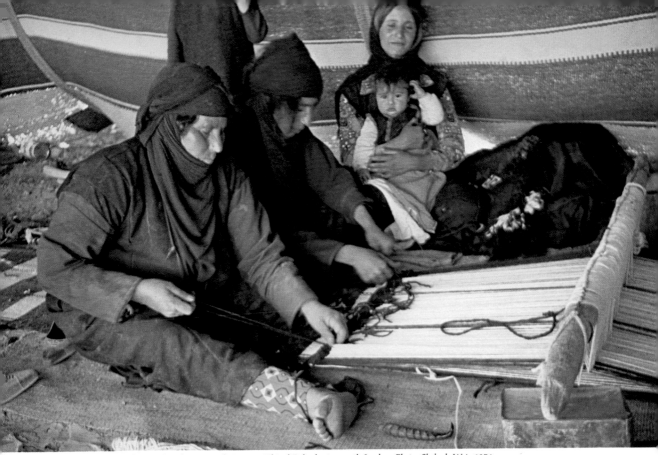

XII. Weaving a rug (*bsāṭ*) with twined weft patterned sections, Dhiyabāt bedouin, south Jordan. *Photo: Shelagh Weir 1974*
XIII. Encampment of the Hamādah at the shrine of Shaykh Hashāsh, southern Sinai. *Photo: Shelagh Weir 1978*

Fig. 62 The 'double dress' (*thōb 'ōb*) of Jordan. This giant-sized dress, over 3 m long, was worn by the bedouin of south Jordan and the Jordan Valley during the last century and the first part of the twentieth century, and is still worn by some of the older women of the town of al-Salt today. The excess material was pulled through a belt so as to hang over in a fold (*'ōb*) above the hem of the dress.
Photo: Shelagh Weir 1968

These are worn with their pointed sleeves turned inside out and tied at the back to reveal the sleeves of gaily patterned underdresses.

The costumes worn by the bedouin women in northern and southern Palestine (part of Israel since 1948) were made from similar materials to those described above, but were normal in size and different in style. From the late nineteenth century, the dresses of women in the Negev desert were embroidered in coloured cross-stitch on the chest and skirt in imitation of village women's dresses. There were, however, distinctive bedouin stitches, patterns and colours. One feature not found in village dresses is the use of blue embroidery by unmarried girls and women past child-bearing age.

Marital status was indicated by caps (*ugā*) of red striped satin decorated with coins, and in the western Negev by bands of coins (*burga'*) worn over the face. The head was covered by a blue or black cotton veil, and was sometimes decorated with red appliqué edging or embroidery for ceremonial wear. This contrasted with the white head veils of the village women. Negev women also wore a distinctive woollen girdle they plaited themselves. This has two parts: a broad grey and black striped under-girdle, and a narrower black sash with coloured chevron patterns and fringed and tasselled ends which was worn over it. Colourful woollen bands were hung from this girdle for festive occasions.

The dresses still worn by the Galilee bedouin have narrow sleeves, and bands of lace-like running-stitch embroidery above the hem, and early this century were worn with tablet-woven woollen girdles. These dresses, with their distinctive embroidery, are in marked contrast to the costumes of the Galilee villagers, but bear strong similarities to those of the villagers of north Jordan and southern Syria with whom the Galilee bedouin have social and economic connections.

For outings women wear a black cotton jacket (*damer*) embroidered in red, though jackets were once made from blue woollen broadcloth decorated with red silk cord. The head is covered with a black crepe veil (*milfa'*) and bound with a silk headband (*'aṣbeh*) with metallic brocade, similar to those worn in Jordan.

Below Fig. 63 Decorative bands, Negev desert. Multi-coloured wool and white cotton in twined weft weave. A number of these bands are suspended from their belts by the women of the Beersheba area for festive occasions.
Max. L. 71 cm. 1975 AS7 9, 10 and 11

Below, right Fig. 64 Woman of the 'Azāzmeh bedouin, Negev desert, wearing a plaited woollen girdle decorated with cowrie shells.
Photo: Klaus-Otto Hundt 1975

Above Fig. 65 Back skirt panel of the dress illustrated in Fig. 66.

Right Fig. 66 Dress (*thōb*) worn by the bedouin of the Beersheba area, Negev desert. Black cotton with cross stitch embroidery in multi-coloured silks. The embroidery of this area is strongly influenced by that of the village women of south Palestine in its designs and its distribution on the dress. Before European embroidery silks came on the market, red was the predominant embroidery colour for married women, and blue for unmarried and old women.
L. 1.5 m, max. W. 1.28 m. 1971 AS 1 8

Men's costume

Until about the middle of this century the traditional costume of bedouin men throughout the Palestine/Jordan area consisted of a long white robe (*thōb*), a wide sleeveless cloak (*'abāyeh*), a head veil (*keffīyeh*) and head-ropes (*'agāl*). (But men's fashions have also changed. For example, head-ropes were much thicker in the last century than they are today, and European-style jackets are now widely worn, often instead of the *'abāyeh*.) Over the *thōb* a leather cartridge belt, or a tablet-woven belt, made in Damascus, was worn. For special occasions a long sleeved coat (*gumbāz, kibber*) of satin (*atlas*) was worn over the *thōb*. The cloak for everyday wear was woven from wool and often striped. Cloaks of cotton or fine wool were worn in summer. A man of high status would wear a cloak of fine quality camel hair or silk cloth embroidered round the neck with metal thread, head-ropes with sections of silver or gold thread, and an elaborate silver dagger. A coat (*furwah*) of broadcloth lined with fleece was also worn in winter.

See Weir, 1989, for further information on women's and men's costume.

Fig. 68 Izzat al-Aṭawneh, a young bedouin shaykh of
the Aṭawneh bedouin, wearing head-ropes ('agāl)
ornamented with metal wire, and a dagger decorated
with niello patterns. Negev desert, Palestine, early
twentieth century.

Fig. 67 Man wearing the fleece-lined winter coat
(*furwah*) made in the cities and worn by the bedouin
in winter.

Photo: William Lancaster 1973

Jewellery

A bedouin woman appreciates jewellery for its ornamental value, but it is also important to her in other ways. She normally acquires her first jewellery collection at marriage and it remains an outward sign of her new marital status. It also represents her own share in her marriage transaction. Her jewellery is either part of the brideprice paid by the groom to her father, or is bought for her by her father after he receives the brideprice. In either case, the jewellery is entirely her own property. If she needs cash she can sell part of it, or if she earns money she can add to it. In this way she can bank her capital in a portable commodity which has intrinsic value, and which experience has shown will keep its true worth. Certain pieces of jewellery are also thought to have protective and beneficial effects on the wearer, and particularly popular among bedouin women is jewellery which combines talismanic with decorative functions.

The bride is never involved in the purchasing of the jewellery, and may not even know that her marriage is about to take place. Bedouin camped near a town visit the silversmith's shop to buy the jewellery, while those camped in the desert buy from itinerant craftsmen and traders who travel round the bedouin camps with their wares. Formerly gypsies (*nuwār*) made a living in this way.

All the jewellery illustrated here was fashionable among the bedouin women of the Palestine/Jordan area during the first half of this century. Similar styles may have been worn in the nineteenth century and earlier, but we have no means of knowing. Every town had its silversmiths who made the jewellery for all the people in their locality. Where there was a mixed population of townspeople, villagers and bedouin, they would all wear similar jewellery produced by the same silversmiths. The main differences would be in the value of the pieces. As bedouin were usually poorer than the settled peoples, the silversmiths provided for them cheaper items of lower grade silver.

The jewellery styles of this area have been subjected to many influences. Jewellery brought back from the Hajj and imported by Christian and Muslim pilgrims to Palestine must have been the source of many new ideas. Other innovations in technique and design were brought in by foreign silversmiths who were attracted by the relative prosperity of the Levant. Many of the silversmiths working in Transjordan and Palestine early this century were from outside: Syrians, Hejāzis, Armenians,

Fig. 69 Girl of the 'Azāzmeh bedouin wearing bead necklaces, hair pins decorated with coins, and a gold nose ring (*shnāf*).
Photo: Shelagh Weir 1974

Fig. 70 Yusef Faghāl, a silversmith who came to Jordan from Medina, Saudi Arabia, with the Emir Abdullah's expedition in 1921. He worked in Madaba, Amman and Kerak, where he now lives, and was one of the craftsmen responsible for introducing Hejāzi tehniques and styles of jewellery to Jordan.
Photo: Shelagh Weir 1974

Circassians and Yemenites. It is also interesting to note that silversmiths were often members of religious minorities: Christians or Jews. Two of the jewellery techniques in use during this period are remembered as having been introduced by foreign silversmiths. In the 1920s jewellery decorated with soldered pieces and granulation appeared. This technique is said to have been brought to the area by a group of Hejāzi silversmiths who came to Transjordan with the Emir Abdullah in 1921. Later, jewellery decorated with black niello became popular, a technique attributed to the Circassian and Armenian silversmiths who settled in Transjordan from the late nineteenth century onwards. Bracelets with niello decoration are still called *asāwir sirkez*, meaning 'Circassian bracelet', in south

Fig. 71 Small charms (*ḥijāb*) worn by children and adults to protect them from dangers and illnesses.
Left: Red stone inscribed with Arabic script, set in silver with silver pendants and coins.
Centre: Blue ceramic bead set in silver with silver pendants.
Right: Light brown bead, possibly amber, with shallow incised markings, set in base metal with pendant base metal imitation coins and a figure resembling a frog. Many stones and beads are thought to have particular powers. For example, the blue bead is thought to provide protection against the evil eye, red stones to ensure good health, and a milky-white stone to promote successful lactation in nursing mothers.
L., from left to right, 9 cm, 10 cm and 7 cm.
1971 AS1 79, 81 and 78

Jordan. The reason given for the great popularity of niello is that the customer could be sure that jewellery was made from a high quality silver if it had niello decoration, for it would not take on low grade metal. Filigree work probably came originally from Yemen. There were a number of Yemenite Jewish silversmiths working in Palestine and the Jordan area from the late nineteenth century, long before the mass exodus of Jews from Yemen around 1950. Silversmiths were extremely jealous of their technical expertise and the secrets of their craft were closely guarded within their families.

In the late 1930s silver jewellery began to go out of fashion and was replaced by gold, a process which seems to have taken place more gradually in Transjordan than in Palestine. The reason for this change can be understood in the context of the social and economic importance of jewellery. During the period of British rule the area became more prosperous. Goods became more expensive, the brideprice rose along with other prices and the value of the bridal jewellery rose proportionately. At the same time, the old sources of silver – Maria Theresa dollars and Turkish riyals – dried up, and gold became more easily available. Few silversmiths seem to have been able

to adapt to the new material, and the manufacture of gold jewellery became centred in the cities: mainly in Damascus and Beirut. The interaction between the ideas and talents of the individual craftsman and the tastes and needs of the customer disappeared, and gold jewellery was mass produced in uniform styles. Today all the younger bedouin women wear gold jewellery, or gold coins strung on a ribbon round their necks or on a band round their foreheads, and many of the older women have now sold their silver and exchanged it for gold.

Fig. 73 Amulet (*māskeh*) of silver, inscribed with the name of Allah. Attached to the chain are two tubular silver boxes (*khiyārah*, literally 'cucumber'). Such containers are often called amulet cases, although they rarely contain anything. Said by one silversmith to have been made in al-Salt, Jordan, by a Syrian craftsman.
L. 33 cm, D. of amulet 5.5 cm. 1975 AS3 25

Fig. 72 Small charms (*hijāb*).
Left: a silver rosette in the centre of which a blue bead, against the evil eye, was probably mounted.
Right: the tooth of an animal mounted in silver. Certain animals' teeth and bones are thought to give protection against misfortune.
L. 6 cm and 10 cm. 1971 AS1 83, 1975 AS3 50

Fig. 75 Amulets (*māskeh*) of silver wih niello
decoration, and pendant sand-cast ornaments and
coins. Worn round the neck on silver chains, these
amulets were fashionable among the bedouin
women in Jordan until twenty or thirty years ago.
Made by jewellers in Kerak, Amman and Irbid.
L., left to right, 21 cm, 11 cm, 13 cm.
Left to right: 1971 AS1 71 and 70 and 1975 AS3 18

Fig. 74 Amulets (*māskeh*) of
hammered silver with incised
decoration and Arabic script,
some very crudely applied.
Amulets such as these were made
by itinerant silversmiths who
visited bedouin camps and
worked and sold their wares on
the spot.
L., 12 cm, 6 cm, 5 cm, 6 cm.
Top: 1971 AS 1 68
Bottom: 1975 AS3 23, 21 and 20

Techniques

The following techniques for working silver were in use
among the silversmiths of the Palestine/Jordan area during the
first part of this century.

Hammering (ṭariq)

The silver is hammered into flat sheets then cut and/or bent to
the required shape, and soldered as necessary. This technique
is often combined with engraving.

Repoussé (ḍarab shakūsh)

A sheet of silver is laid on a bed of pitch and hammered with
variously shaped punches, or it is hammered onto a shaped
mould. In either case the design appears in relief on the
reverse side of the work.

Fig. 76 Detail from a silver chain (*jnād*).
Total L. 1.08 m. 1975 AS3 16.

Fig. 77 Amulet (*ḥijāb*) in the form of a rectangular box in silver with niello decoration, and pendant sand-cast ornaments and coins. The chain also has sand-cast ornaments at intervals. These boxes are often called amulet cases, but there is usually only wadding inside. Made in Jordan and worn round the neck by bedouin women up to thirty or forty years ago.
L. including chain 55 cm, L. of amulet 12.5 cm. 1971 AS1 66

Fig. 80 Bracelet (*asāwir sirkez*).
D. 6 cm. 1975 AS3 46

Previous page. Top Fig. 78 Amulet
Previous page. Top Fig. 78 Amulet
(*ḥijāb*) in the form of a fish, Jordan.
Silver with relief decoration made
by the sand-casting technique
from an original made by the
filigree technique. The diamond-
shaped ornaments may have been
applied after casting. The baubles
attached to the chain are probably
a later addition. The eye socket
would have contained a blue bead
(against the evil eye). The
decoration of this piece shows
Hejāzi influence, and it was
probably made by one of the
Hejāzi jewellers such as Yusef
Faghāl or his predecessors.
L. 8 cm. 1975 AS3 17

Bottom Fig. 79 Amulets (*samakah*)
in the form of fishes, Jordan.
Silver with niello decoration, the
centre amulet with sand-cast
pendant ornaments, the others
with pendant coins. The fish is a
very old decorative motif in the
Middle East. Although it may
once have been a fertility symbol,
neither the women who wore
these ornaments during the 1920s
and 1930s nor the silversmiths
who made them, attributed any
special significance to the shape.
L. of fish 8–9.5 cm. 1971 AS1 73, 74 and 72

Filigree (qisr shift or mshabbak)

Qisr shift roughly translated means 'forced with pliers' and
mshabbak means 'netted'. Filigree is the twisting and soldering
together of wire to make various patterns. This technique is
commonly used for baubles and relief decoration on a plain or
engraved silver base.

Granulation (shughl al-khurduq or habbīyāt)

The soldering (*talḥīm*) of small silver granules, or other shapes,
particularly diamonds, onto a silver base. When the granules
are in clusters they are called 'mulberry seeds' (*habbāt al-tūt*).
This technique is often combined with filigree work.

Sand casting (sakib)

A mould is made by pressing the model between a pair of iron
frames packed tightly with very fine sand (*raml*). The sand is
treated with a mixture of alum, salt and sugar in water so as to
retain the exact impression of the model when it is removed. A
copy is then cast from this mould (which can be used only
once). This technique can be used to copy pieces made by any
of the other techniques.

Niello (mḥabbar)

Mḥabbar derives from the word for ink and refers to the black
colour of the niello (a combination of silver, copper and lead
sulphides). The powdered niello is placed in etched or cast
recesses in the silver ornament, then melted and filed to make
a smooth surface.

Chainmaking

A variety of chains (*sinsāl*) were made, with different types of
links, spacers and baubles combining the techniques of filigree, granulation and sandcasting.

The main source of silver coins: Maria Theresa dollars (called
abu rīsheh, literally 'father of feathers' because of the wings
depicted on the obverse) which contained about eighty per
cent silver, Turkish riyals which had a lower silver content,
and base metal coins for cheap jewellery. The best quality
jewellery contained about eighty per cent silver. The main
alloy used was copper which was said to give the best sheen.

The jewellery

The following items of jewellery were worn by bedouin women in Palestine and the Jordan area up to the 1940s, and were made by silversmiths working in Nablus, Jerusalem, Bethlehem, Hebron, Beersheba, Gaza, Irbid, Amman, Madaba, al-Salt and Kerak.

Amulets

(a) Stones and beads, sometimes set in silver. Many colours and types, each one effective against a particular ill. For example, a bottle green stone (*kharazet al-kabseh*) against postnatal disease in a mother, a smooth white stone (*kharazet al-ḥalīb*) to promote lactation in nursing mothers, and a blue bead (*'owayneh*) against the evil eye.

(b) Oval in shape (*māskeh*). Plain hammered silver with engraved patterns or Quranic inscriptions, and with niello decoration.

(c) Rectangular boxes (*ḥijāb*) with niello decoration.

(d) Cylindrical boxes (*khiyārah*).

(e) Fish-shaped amulets (*samakah*), filigree, sand cast or decorated with niello.

Necklaces

(a) Chains (bedouin: *jarīr*, townspeople: *sinsāl*). Various kinds: links with floral ornaments at intervals (*sinsāl farkeh*), rods at intervals (*sinsāl 'amūd*), and with baubles and balls attached (*jnād*). Some very long, reaching to the waist, some worn under one arm, and others shorter with amulets pendant from them.

(b) Choker (*kirdān*), silver ornaments and pendants on a cotton band. Made with a variable number of silver ornaments to suit the pocket of the customer.

(c) Necklaces (*'oqd mirjān*) of coral with amber and mother of pearl spacers.

(d) Necklaces of cylindrically-shaped amber beads.

Bracelets

(a) Broad or narrow with niello decoration, always worn in pairs one on each wrist (*asāwir sirkez, sirān sarsak*).

(b) Shaped amber beads.

Fig. 81 Necklace (*gilādet al-krunful*), Negev desert. A choker of various kinds and colours of beads, and pendant from it three multiple strings of cloves interspersed with beads, coral and mother-of-pearl spacers. The strings terminate with blue, maroon and orange silk tassels, each strand ending in a tiny glass bead.
L. 53 cm. 1975 AS3 31

Fig. 82 Necklace (*kirdān*), Jordan. Silver ornaments attached to a textile band, and silver sand-cast ornaments and coins pendant from it. Made in Irbid, Kerak and Nablus (Palestine) up to about thirty years ago, and worn by both bedouin and village women. *L. of necklace 32 cm. 1975 AS3 15*

Fig. 83 Pair of silver bracelets (*asāwir mīnā*), Jordan. Ornamented with niello with a hinged opening and pin fastening, they are unusually broad and were made, according to one informant, by an Armenian silversmith called Rubīn who worked in Jerusalem during the British Mandate period. *H. 6 cm, W. 6.5 cm. 1975 AS3 48*

Above Fig. 84 Pair of silver bracelets (*saba'awīyāt*),
Negev desert. Decorated in relief by the hammering
technique (repoussé). One worn on each wrist.
W. 6.5 cm. 1975 AS3 41a and b

Right Fig. 85 Pair of silver bracelets (*maṣrīyeh*), Negev
desert. Made by silversmiths in Egypt (mainly Jewish).
W. 6.5 cm. 1975 AS3 44a and b

Fig. 86 Forehead ornament (*kaffāt* or
khamasīyāt), Jordan and Palestine.
Hand-shaped ornaments of low
grade metal pendant from a chain.
Worn around the forehead by the
women of the Ta'āmreh and
'Obaydiyeh groups of semi-settled
bedouin in the Jordan Valley and
Bethlehem area. Made by jewellers
in Jerusalem during the first half of
this century.
L. 38 cm. 1975 AS3 28

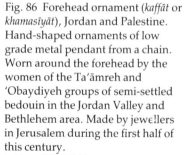

Rings (khawātem)

Various stones set in silver, or plain silver rings. Up to four
worn on each hand.

Hairpins (bukleh)

Usually decorated with niello.

Forehead ornament (kaffāt or khamasiyāt)

Worn by the semi-settled bedouin of the Jordan valley area.

Nose rings (shnāf or zmaymah)

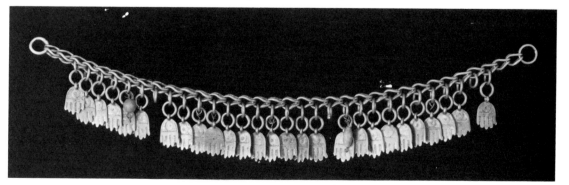

Fig. 87 Gold nose ring (*shnāf*) worn by bedouin
women in the Negev desert.
W. 3.5 cm. 1975 AS3 29

Fig. 88 Negev bedouin woman in Khan Yunis
wearing a band of coins (*burga'*) over her face. Coins
are used as ornaments on the head and face to a
greater extent in the Negev desert than in the area
east of the Jordan valley.
Photo: Shelagh Weir 1967

Select Annotated Bibliography

Abou-Zeid, Ahmed M. 1965. (ed. J. G. Peristiany) 'Honour and shame among the bedouins of Egypt', in *Honour and Shame: the values of Mediterranean society*. London: Weidenfeld & Nicolson: 243–59.

Abu Lughod, Laila 1987. *Veiled Sentiments*. Berkeley: University of California Press.
On the bedouin women of the Western desert of Egypt, and their self-expression through poetry and song.

al-'Ārif, 'Ārif 1944. *Bedouin love, law and legend*. Jerusalem: Cosmos. English version, with changes, of *Al-qaḍā' bayn al-badū* (1933). (Also published in German.)
A study of the legal theory and practice of the bedouin of Beersheba.

Ashkenazi, Tovia 1938. *Tribus semi-nomades de la Palestine du nord*. Paris: Paul Geuthner.
Ethnographic survey of eighty groups in north Palestine.

Bailey, Clinton 1990. *Bedouin Poetry from Sinai and the Negev*. Oxford: Oxford University Press.

Bates, Daniel and A. Rassam 1983. *Peoples and Cultures of the Middle East*. New Jersey: Prentice Hall. (Chapter 5)

Boucheman, Albert de 1935. *Matériel de la vie bédouine recueilli dans le désert de Syrie (tribus des Arabes Sba'a)*. Documents d'Etudes Orientales, 3. Paris: Institut Français de Damas.

Burkhardt, J. L. 1830. (ed. Sir W. Ouseley) *Notes on the Bedouins and the Wahabys*. London: Henry Coburn & Richard Bentley. Reprint 1967: New York.

Charles, H. 1939. *Tribus moutonnières du moyen-Euphrate*. Documents d'Etudes Orientales. Beirut: Institut Français de Damas.

Chatty, Dawn 1986. *From Camel to Truck: the Bedouin in the Modern World*. New York: Vantage Press.
Describes how Syrian bedouin maintain their traditional way of life herding animals in the desert while integrating into the modern economy of their region.

Cole, Donald Powell 1975. *Nomads of the nomads. The Āl Murrah bedouin of the Empty Quarter*. Chicago: Aldine Publishing Co.

Coon, Carleton S. 1952. *Caravan: the story of the Middle East*. London: Jonathan Cape.
Classic anthropological study of the area.

Crichton, Anne-Rhona 1989. *Al-Sadu: the Techniques of Bedouin Weaving*. Kuwait: Al Sadu.
Detailed descriptions, photographs and diagrams of weaving techniques and textiles.

Crowfoot, Grace Mary 1921. 'Spinning and weaving in the Sudan', in *Sudan Notes and Records*, 4 (1): 20–38. Khartoum.

Crowfoot, Grace Mary 1931. *Methods of hand spinning in Egypt and the Sudan*. Halifax: Bankfield Museum Notes, 2nd Series: 12.

Crowfoot, Grace Mary 1934. 'The mat looms of Huleh, Palestine', in *Palestine Exploration Fund Quarterly*.

Crowfoot, Grace Mary 1941. 'The vertical loom in Palestine and Syria', in *Palestine Exploration Quarterly*, October.

Crowfoot, Grace Mary 1944a. 'Handicrafts in Palestine: primitive weaving (1) Plaiting and finger weaving', in *Palestine Exploration Quarterly*, July–October: 121–30.

Crowfoot, Grace Mary 1944b. 'Handicrafts in Palestine: Jerusalem hammock cradles and Hebron rugs', in *Palestine Exploration Quarterly*, January–April: 121–30.

Crowfoot, Grace Mary 1945. 'The tent beautiful: a study of pattern weaving in Trans-Jordan' in *Palestine Exploration Quarterly*, January–April: 34–47.

Dalman, Gustaf Hermann 1928–42. *Arbeit und Sitte in Palästina*, vol. VI. Gütersloh: C. Bertelsman. Reprint 1967: Hildesheim.

Dickson, H. R. P. 1948. *The Arab of the desert: a glimpse into the bedawin life in Kuwait and Saudi Arabia*. London: Allen and Unwin.
On the domestic life of the Shammar and 'Anazah tribes, and the Muntafiq shepherd tribes and outcast Salubbah tribe.

Dickson, H. R. P. 1956. *Kuwait and her neighbours*. London: Allen and Unwin.
On the history of Kuwait with details of the tribes, especially the 'Ajman bedouin.

Diqs, Isaak 1967. *A Bedouin Boyhood*. London: Allen and Unwin.
Autobiographical account by a Jordanian bedouin educated in the Western tradition.

Dostal, Walter 1967. *Die Beduinen in Südarabien. Eine ethnologische Studie zur Entwicklung der Kamelwirtenkultur in Arabien*. Vienna: Berger (illus.).
Ethnographical study of the bedouin in south Arabia and the development of the camel herding culture.

Doughty, Charles 1885. *Travels in Arabia Deserta*. 2 vols. London: Jonathan Cape.

Eickleman, Dale 1989. *The Middle East: an Anthropological Approach* (2nd edition). Englewood Cliffs: Prentice Hall.
(Chapter 4)

Evans-Prichard, E. E. 1949. *The Sanusi of Cyrenaica*. Oxford: Clarendon Press.
On the development of the Sanusi religious order among the bedouin.

Feilberg, C. G. 1944. *La tente noire: contribution ethnographique à l'histoire des nomades*. Copenhagen: Nationalmuseeta Skrifter. Ethnografisk. Roekke II.
Discusses the construction and distribution of the tent in Arabia, Asia and north Africa.

Fernea, Robert A. 1970. *Shaykh and Effendi: changing patterns of authority among the el-Shabana of southern Iraq*. Cambridge, Mass.: Harvard University Press.
On settled agriculturalists descended from bedouin.

Freer, A. M. Goodrich (H. H. Spoer) 1924. *Arabs in Tent and Town: An intimate account of the family life of the Arabs of Syria with a description of the animals and plants of their country*. London: Seeley, Service and Co. Photographs.

Falah, Ghazi 1983. *The Role of the British Administration in the Sedentarization of Bedouin Tribes in Northern Palestine, 1918–1948*. Durham: University of Durham.

Hecht, Ann 1989. *The Art of the Loom*. London: British Museum Publications.
Chapter 2 is on bedouin weaving.

Ingham, Bruce 1986. *Bedouin of North Arabia*. London: Jonathan Cape.
Focuses on bedouin poetry.

Jarvis, Claude S. 1931. *Yesterday and Today in Sinai*. Edinburgh and London.

Jaussen, P. Antonin 1908. *Coûtumes des Arabes au Pays de Moab*. Paris. Reprint 1948: Paris: Adrien-Maisonneuve.

Jennings-Bramley, W. S. 1905–14. 'The bedouin of the Sinaitic Peninsula', in *Palestine Exploration Quarterly* (various issues).

Kennet, A. 1925. *Beduin Justice: laws and customs among the Egyptian beduin*. Cambridge.

Lancaster, William 1981. *The Rwala Bedouin Today*. Cambridge: Cambridge University Press.
A detailed study of social change among the Rwala of Syria and northern Saudi Arabia.

Lavie, Smadar 1990. *The Poetics of Military Occupation*. Berkeley: University of California Press.
On the Mzeina bedouin in southern Sinai under Egyptian and Israeli administrations.

Lawrence, T. E. 1935. *Seven Pillars of Wisdom*. London: Jonathan Cape.
On the Arab Revolt in the Great War with descriptions of bedouin personalities and customs.

Maddrell, Penny with **Yunis al-Grinawi** 1990. *The Beduin of the Negev*. London: Minority Rights Group Report No. 81.
Examination of the economic and political problems of bedouin in the context of the Israeli-Palestinian conflict.

Marx, Emanuel 1967. *Bedouin of the Negev*. Manchester: Manchester Univerity Press.

Marx, Emanuel and **Avshalom Shmueli** (eds) 1984. *The Changing Bedouin*. London: Transaction Books.
Case studies detailing the cultural, economic and legal changes taking place among the bedouin of the Negev and Sinai deserts.

Montagne, R. 1947. *La civilisation du désert: nomades d'Orient de d'Afrique*. Paris: Le Tour du Monde.
On Saudi tribes, especially the Shammar.

Murray, G. W. 1935. *Sons of Ishmael: A study of the Egyptian beduin*. London: George Routledge & Sons (illus.). Reprint 1967.
Based on 25 years' surveying experience.

Musil, Alois 1908. *Arabia Petraea*, 3 vols (in German). Vienna.
Vol. 3 on the nomads of Jordan (Transjordan).

Musil, Alois 1928. *The manners and customs of the Rwala bedouins*. New York: American Geographical Society.
6. Information collected in 1908–9.

Nelson, C. 1973. *The Desert and the Sown: nomads in the wider society*. Berkeley: Institute of International Studies, University of California.

Oppenheim, Max von 1949–68. *Die Beduinen*, 4 vols. Leipzig and Wiesbaden: Unter Mitbearbeitung von Erich Braunlich und Werner Caskel. Bibliography.
Comprehensive work on bedouin genealogies and territories.

Peters, Emrys L. 1990. (eds J. Goody and E. Marx) *The Bedouin of Cyrenaica: Studies in Personal and Corporate Power*. Cambridge: Cambridge University Press.
Compilation of Peters' major published and unpublished articles on the Cyrenaican bedouin of Libya.

Raswan, Carl R. 1947. *The Black Tents of Arabia (my life amongst the beduins)*. New York: Creative Age Press. (Also published in German, 1934) Glossary.
On the Rwala bedouins.

Salem-Murdock, Muneera 1989. *Arabs and Nubians in New Halfa*. Salt Lake City: University of Utah Press.
On populations re-settled in the Egyptian-Sudanese border region as a result of the building of the Aswan Dam.

Salzman, Philip Carl (ed.) 1980. *When Nomads Settle: Processes of Sedentarisation as Adaptation and Response*. New York: Praeger.
On nomads in various parts of Africa and the Middle East, including several contributions on the bedouin.

Stein, Lothar. 1967. *Die Šammar-Ǧerba. Bedouinen im übergang von Nomadismus zur Sesshaftigkeit*. Berlin: Akademie Verlag.
On the settlement of the nomadic Shammar tribes on agriculturally marginal land.

Stewart, Frank 1988. *Texts in Sinai Bedouin Law, Part 1*. Mediterranean Language and Culture Monograph Series Part 5, Wiesbaden: Harrassovitz.

Sweet, Louise E. (ed.) 1970. *Depth and Diversity*, Vol. I of *The Central Middle East: an anthropological reader*. New York: Natural History Press.
Collection of articles including by Doughty (1936), Sweet (1965) and Peters (1960).

Sweet, Louise E. 1971. *The Central Middle East: A handbook of anthropology and published research on the Nile Valley, the Arab Levant, southern Mesopotamia, the Arabian peninsula and Israel.* New Haven: Human relations Area Files.
Especially relevant: L. E. Sweet, 'The Arabian Peninsula', 271–355.

Thesiger, W. 1959. *Arabian Sands.* London: Longman.
Record of journeys in 1945–50. Includes information on the pastoral tribes of the Empty Quarter.

Weir, Shelagh 1970. *Spinning and Weaving in Palestine.* London: British Museum.

Weir, Shelagh 1975. 'Some observations on pottery and weaving in the Yemen Arab Republic', in *Proceedings of the Seminar for Arabian Studies*, 5: 65–76. London.

Weir, Shelagh 1989. *Palestinian Costume.* London: British Museum Publications.
Includes descriptions and illustrations of the costumes of Galilee and Negev bedouin men and women.

Fig. 89 Bedouin driving a tractor, Wadi Musa area, south Jordan.
Photo: Shelagh Weir 1975